D1527872

CRYSTALS AND GEMSTONES FOR KIDS AND TEENS

A BEGINNER'S GUIDE TO THE HEALING AND SELF-CARE MAGIC OF CRYSTALS, GEMS AND STONES—INCLUDING CHAKRA AND ZODIAC/ASTROLOGY CRYSTALS—WITH THEIR MEANINGS

ALLEGRA GRANT

GO PUBLISHING

CONTENTS

INTRODUCTION

"What's your favorite crystal?"

The text was from my shy, artsy, sensitive, super-cool 14-year-old niece, Haley. The expression on my face could only be described as a giant smile, mixed with a full jaw-drop.

Me: "My favorite crystal changes! But today I've been carrying my Rose Quartz."

Haley: "OMG. Rose Quartz is MY favorite!"

And that's how it began...

Over the next year and a half, mostly by text, but sometimes by FaceTime, my niece and I bonded over our mutual love of crystals. I'd grab a few for her each time I went to the crystal shop. She'd pick my brain about how to use them, and I'd give her tips. By the time she was preparing for her Sweet Sixteen, she was a full-fledged crystal girl. Like me!

Plus, BONUS: we forged a really great friendship along the way.

Hi! My name is Allegra. I live in New York City with my husband and our rescue dog Cliff. I'm a writer, a pretty good baker, a terrible singer, and I'm obsessed with crystals. I've been using them in my daily life for years, and I love nothing more than sharing everything I've learned about them.

And so, with my niece Haley in mind, I decided to write a book for you: a young person who is just starting your journey into the magical world of crystals, and hopefully discovering all the wonderful ways that crystals can improve your life.

Haley, like I said, is almost sixteen. She's amazing! She's smart, funny, an incredible singer, and a really great friend. You'll be getting to know her—and me—throughout this book as we show you some of our favorite crystals. And teach you how to use them.

By the end of this book, I hope you will be a fully fledged crystal guy or girl, just like Haley and me.

We have loved learning about crystals together and want you to have all the benefits, too.

If you don't have any crystals yet—no problem! We will start at the beginning. If you already have a few —even better! In this book, I'll tell you everything I've learned about crystals: through research, through talking with other crystal fans like me, and through my own trial and error. It's been incredible to learn all this, and I'm so excited to share it with you! You can join me and Haley on your own, or maybe you have a friend or family member you want to bring along for the ride. Either way is okay, and we are so happy to have you here.

But first, here is a list of things that crystals can do. (I'm about to blow your mind a little bit.)

Crystals can...

- help you when you're nervous...
- give you energy when you can't even...
- sharpen your brain when you're studying...
- teach you how to communicate better with your friends and your parents...
- fill your heart with a love that is infectious...

Plus, much, much, much more.

There is so much I have learned, and I'm going to teach you some of it in this book. So you can learn to be a crystal girl, too (or crystal guy...or crystal nonbinary person...or whatever kind of crystal person you personally choose to be).

For me, one of the coolest things about being a crystal girl is how aware it's made me of the planet and everyone on it. Before I was into crystals, I took everything for granted, as just part of life. If I saw a rock on the side of the road, well, I probably didn't even notice it in the first place. Or, if I did, I just thought of it as, well, a rock.

Now I see the world as a place filled with wonder and movement. And it's really exciting.

Of course, when I was little, I was into all kinds of magical things. I believed in unicorns and fairies, and pretty much anything else. If you told me it was real, I believed in it.

Once I grew up, though, I stopped believing in stuff like that. And honestly, I don't know that I necessarily believe in that stuff, still ...but I do believe in crystals.

When I first learned about crystals, I was a skeptic. My friend Flora basically had to drag me to the crystal store, and even then I only went to prove I was cool enough to hang out with someone like her. After a while, though, I started to realize, hey, maybe there's something to this! And I started to notice the big difference it made.

Luckily for Haley, she learned about crystals much younger than I did. This sometimes makes me jealous! (Just kidding. Haley knows I'm joking.)

But seriously, all the help I've gotten from crystals would've come in handy much sooner and saved me lots of stress and worry. Crystals have taught me so much about the kind of person I was meant to be. And they've taught me that it's okay to like myself, just the way I am. Really, I've become a much stronger, happier person since learning about crystals. And that's what I want for you, too!

Are you as excited as I am?! Let's go!!!

Before we dive headlong into choosing crystals, let's take just a few minutes to discuss what crystals are, and why they work. And I have a few warnings too —nothing scary—but just a few no-nos before we really get started to keep you extra safe. Just like in science class when the teacher starts out with some ground rules, I'm going to share everything you need to have a safe and fun adventure in the world of crystal magic. But first, here is a short—and I mean really short   science lesson on crystals.

A SUPER-BRIEF (NOT-TOO-NERDY) SCIENCE LESSON

Have you ever heard the saying, "Everything is energy"? It's from, like, the smartest person who ever lived: Albert Einstein. Without going into a full-on physics lesson, this saying simply means that everything on the planet—your softball mitt, your Social Studies book, your favorite jeans—everything is constantly moving!

That doesn't seem true, right? Your Social Studies book is just sitting in your backpack. But here's the cool thing: Your Social Studies book is actually made up of billions and billions of tiny bits called atoms. And each atom is actually made of even smaller bits that are racing around each other at a super-fast speed all the time. You can't tell by looking it at, but your Social Studies book is actually vibrating, so fast that you can't see it, but it's vibrating, all the same. And that's energy!

I'm vibrating. You're vibrating. Mount Everest is vibrating!

So that means...

I'm made of energy. You're made of energy. Mount Everest is (say it with me) made of energy!

Some things have vibrations that are all over the place, almost like they're wiggling, and shifting, and shaking in unpredictable ways. Have you ever tried to hold a puppy? That's what I'm talking about.

Some things have vibrations that are pretty much always the same. That's because all of the atoms—all of the bits that make those things up—are organized in beautiful, simple, repeating patterns. Think of it like when you make a perfect tower of Legos—all lined up so you create a block that is super-strong.

Crystals are like that block of Legos! With all of the tiny bits lined up in a predictable order. Always perfect. Always the same. Because the little atoms are so neatly organized, the crystal is super strong—and also super pretty. With all those particles in those nice shapes, crystals end up all kinds of fantastic colors, and they also are really durable and hard to destroy.

You can kinda tell just by looking at a crystal that this is true, right? They have beautiful shapes, beautiful colors, beautiful shine...they look like almost nothing else. All of this is because they are perfectly formed, like almost nothing on the whole planet. They're totally unique. That's what makes them so special.

Crystals have a vibration that you can count on!

And more importantly, since the crystals are energy and *you* are energy, you can use crystals to help you through all kinds of things.

Let's say you go to school with a big smile on your face because it's a beautiful day and you're excited to see your friends. Your energy is really positive. But when you get to school, your best friend had a terrible night's sleep. She didn't do her French homework, and she's worried she's going to get detention again. She makes it hard to keep your upbeat, happy attitude, right? It's because your energy and her energy affect each other. You'll probably cheer her up a little, and she'll probably bum you out a little.

That exchange of energy happens all the time!!!!

People are not the only thing that is made of energy, remember? EVERYTHING IS ENERGY. The moon affects the oceans, exchanging energy. A vacuum affects the dirt on the carpet, exchanging energy. And a crystal can affect the person holding it. You can exchange energy with a crystal, and it can exchange energy back with you.

You can give the crystal your bad mood and take from the crystal love, courage, luck, confidence... tons of things.

Discovering how to make the most of this is super-fun, and such a great way to feel connected to, well, the whole world.

So that leads us to the fun part! You can take advantage of these perfect vibrations coming from these gorgeous little rocks! Since the whole planet and everything on it is made of energy, you can use crystals to choose how you want to feel today. It's like a choose-your-own-adventure story, where you collect rocks as you go, and the rocks help you shift your mood at will.

It's incredible, really. This is why I love crystals so much, but you don't have to take my word for it. Here are some examples, and then you can try it for yourself.

Let's get to an example with a beautiful pink crystal called Rose Quartz (my niece's favorite). When you hold a piece of Rose Quartz in your hand, which has the energy of unconditional love, you can't help but feel the positive vibes! It will inspire you to love yourself, other people, your life...your lunch! Everything. It's a little bit of magic you can put in your pocket.

Do you know what unconditional love means? It means the kind of super positive, awesome affection we might get from a best friend or a close family member who lets us know, every day, that no matter what we do, we're still awesome in their eyes. If we make mistakes or forget things or even fly off the handle sometimes, they understand what we're going through and want to let us know we're still important to them. That's the energy of unconditional love, and Rose Quartz just radiates with it.

But wait—How do we know that the energy of a piece of Rose Quartz is the energy of unconditional love? The answer is in the personal stories that people have been sharing about Rose Quartz for literally thousands of years. Ancient Mesopotamians wore jewelry with Rose Quartz to attract love. Ancient Greeks used it to ward off bad luck. Native American tribes used it to help balance their emotions and create a good mood.

Nowadays, right where you live, people are still using Rose Quartz! In yoga studios. In bowls by bathtubs. In rings and necklaces.

And we experience the same magic.

I guess it's correct to say we don't know why Rose Quartz is the crystal of unconditional love, but so many people have experienced the same benefits, over centuries, all over the planet, that we just know. People have spent so much time working with Rose Quartz and noticing how it makes them feel that it's pretty obvious by now what it can do for you. And it can really help you feel good about yourself, even when you mess up.

This is why it's one of my favorites, and it's definitely Haley's favorite, too. We can all use a little extra unconditional love in our life, as that's what makes us feel safe and happy to do and be ourselves, no matter what. When I feel safe to be myself, I'm more confident, I have more fun, and I do better at everything I try because I'm not quite so worried about messing up. Messing up is okay, because we can always learn from our mistakes, say "sorry" if we need to, and do better next time. And Rose Quartz teaches us that it's all fine and good to still love ourselves through the whole process.

That doesn't mean we just do whatever we want without thinking about other people's feelings. Rose Quartz actually helps us care about other people even more than usual, because we understand *them* even better, too. We know they are just people, like us, and they are also just doing their best. Rose Quartz reminds us that we're all one human family, and we can be patient and loving even when it feels hard sometimes.

This is why crystals are so powerful. And that's just one example. Every crystal radiates with all kinds of awesome energies, such as unconditional love, or confidence, or honesty, or courage...the list goes on and on. And it's a really, really cool list.

In the next couple of chapters, I'll share with you some of the most popular crystals and what people experience when they use them. And you can try them all for yourself.

You get to write the next chapter in the history book of crystals. A book that is centuries old and written in hundreds of languages by people from every part of the planet.

It's giving me goose bumps just to imagine that. How about you?

A COUPLE OF TEENY WARNINGS

I do have a couple of things I want to point out. This will be quick.

Some crystals can actually be harmful and toxic. Don't put them in your mouth. And don't leave them around where your younger siblings can put them in their mouths. Most are perfectly harmless, but a few can make people sick if used incorrectly. Don't worry, I'll stick to the safe ones in this book. And if you're worried, you can always google the crystal and see what's up.

Some crystals, like Citrine and Amethyst, shouldn't be left in direct sunlight because their bright colors will fade, and they will turn all pale and weird-looking, which is always such a shame!! Again, I'll give you warnings as we go along.

Other crystals like Kyanite and Malachite shouldn't ever get wet because they'll start to break down or rust, and then little bits of rock dust might get everywhere and cause a mess or even get where we don't want it—like your cat's food bowl. It's really important to treat crystals with respect! So I'll let you know which ones to be extra careful with, but for the most part, crystals are best used as jewelry or decoration, and in the specific ways I will show you in this book. Don't worry, you'll be a crystal pro in no time! I learned really fast, and so did Haley.

One last thing: You don't need to spend tons of money to be a crystal girl or guy. A giant, beautifully carved piece of Lepidolite could cost a few hundred dollars. But you can get the same benefits from the $3 chunk of Lepidolite you find in a tray at the crystal shop. You don't have to empty your savings account to enjoy crystals. You just need a few bucks.

And that's it for the warnings!

ONE FINAL NOTE: HATERS, BACK OFF!

Not everyone believes in crystals. You will probably encounter people who think they're silly. You might even be one of those people right now, and that's okay. But give it a shot. Start with one crystal—they only cost a few dollars—and see what you experience. I firmly believe that if you try to feel the energy of a crystal with all of your heart, that you will absolutely be able to connect with it and get all the benefits.

And if you don't, so what? They're still super pretty and nice to have around. Put them in a little bowl on your nightstand and enjoy looking them. Everybody wins.

CHAPTER 1

THE ONE CRYSTAL YOU SHOULD ABSOLUTELY HAVE

Let's say you have $5 in your pocket, and (miraculously) you find yourself walking past the little crystal shop in your town... It'll probably smell really nice, like essential oils and maybe even incense. It'll probably be filled with really cool fabrics, art, sculpture, and jewelry. But most importantly, it will probably have tons of little baskets of rocks.

Green pointy rocks, blue striped rocks, shiny metallic-looking rocks...which do you choose?

Well, the answer is: Choose the one you like!

Okay, okay. I know that's not an answer you were looking for, but let me explain what I mean, with myself as an example. The first time I walked into a crystal shop, it was because my very, very cool friend

Flora invited me. If I'm being perfectly honest, I thought crystals were kind of dumb. But Flora was always showing me cool stuff, so I gave her the benefit of the doubt.

I decided to just buy one crystal and give it a try. I mean, they are beautiful, right?

And... maybe a crystal might change my life with its magic!

Or maybe it would just be a pretty rock I could keep on my desk.

What was the harm, really?

I had $5 in my pocket, so I looked around.

At that point, I knew absolutely nothing about crystals. And I felt like a big faker walking around and acting like I knew all about them, even though I'd never had a crystal in my life. Flora told me to just keep my mind open. She said one of the crystals would "call to me," which I thought sounded insane. But a cool kind of insane because...well, it was Flora! Everything she does is cool.

Long story short, I picked a beautiful pale blue rock with little dark stripes. I didn't think it "called" to me, but I did think that I liked it.

It was pretty to look at. It felt really nice in my hand when I picked it up. It was within my budget. So I bought it.

That purchase changed my life.

．　．　．

I didn't know it yet, but I had picked up a Blue Lace Agate. It's a crystal that promotes clear and confident communication. I had been struggling to finish a story I'd been writing, and putting that crystal on my desk next to my computer totally changed the energy in the room. I could not explain it, but having the Blue Lace Agate at my side, I had the best day of writing I'd had in months. I was getting the energy of clear and confident communication from a rock! What? How was that even possible?

That day started my journey to becoming the crystal girl (some might say crystal nerd) who is writing this book for you right now.

I used my intuition to find the right crystal. And it changed everything.

So my advice to you is the same advice Flora gave me: for your first crystal: Just look for the stone that is "calling" to you. It might be in a basket of clear rocks called Selenite. It might be in a basket of rough brown and red rocks called Tiger's Eye. Just pick it up and see how it feels. And if it feels good—and is $5 or less—just get it!

And this next part is super important. Don't google the crystal! At least not at first. Spend some time with it. Put it in your pocket. Roll it around in your hand when you're watching TV. Just see what happens.

The universe may have led you to the perfect crystal.

After a day or two, either google the crystal or look it up in this book. When you do a tiny bit of research, you'll be able to learn what the crystal has been used for for thousands of years. Then you can compare it what you've learned with your own personal experience.

- If you picked up Jade, did you experience good luck?
- If you picked up Howlite, did you sleep like a baby?
- If you picked up Citrine, did you feel super hopeful?

I hope you get the chance to try this...and have your mind blown, like mine was.

A quick note: I lied. Just a tiny lie! I did budget $5 to buy a crystal that first day, and I spent $6, instead. I needed to get that off my chest before we went any further. Crystals can do that, sometimes—they are so tempting! So if your allowance isn't much, there are definitely ways to afford crystals. I have started asking for crystals for my birthday, especially if it's a bigger, more expensive one I've been looking for. You know, some people collect baseball cards...I collect crystals! And it's definitely worth it.

. . .

One other note: If you're reading this and thinking, "What the heck is Allegra talking about? How do you listen for a rock to call you?" that's totally okay. Listening to your intuition takes some time and patience. If you're not a person who thinks like that, fine...I'll just tell you what crystal to buy first right now.

This is officially cheating, by the way! I want you to be able to choose your own crystals, eventually! But I want to help you figure this out. If you need a little push, I can provide that. Then, once you have a little practice, you'll start to recognize which crystals work well for you and which ones don't.

If you identify as female, you cannot go wrong with Rose Quartz, which is a lovely pink. It's got a frequency and vibration that I think is easy to feel. I've mentioned it already, but it's the energy of unconditional love. And that includes love for yourself. Start here. It's a powerful one.

If you identify as male, I'd start with Hematite. It's metallic and shiny, and it's what's known as a grounding crystal. It helps you feel confident because it connects you to the earth and reminds you that all the strength you need is already inside you. Hematite feels great in your hand also. It's heavy and smooth.

If you identify as non-binary, or if you're a person who doesn't like to be defined by gender, pick up some Lepidolite. It's purple or blue with lots of multi-colored specks that always remind me of stars. (You pronounce it lep-PID-o-light, by the way.) Looking into a piece of Lepidolite is like looking into the beauty of outer space. It's incredibly calming, and it reminds you that the universe is full of possibilities. If you sit and look at Lepidolite, you'll know that anything in the whole universe is possible. It's a nice feeling. And when you feel that way, it's sometimes amazing what can happen if you believe it can!

CHAPTER 2

I GOT MY FIRST CRYSTAL. UM, NOW WHAT?

You are on your way! You've got your first crystal.

Maybe it's a crystal that called to you.
Maybe it's one of the crystals I suggested.
Maybe it's a crystal someone gave you as a gift.
Maybe you just ordered one on Amazon.

It really doesn't matter. You're in the game!!
So now what?

Later on in the book, I'm going to tell you some of the really cool/fun/bizarre ways people use their crystals, but in this section, I'm just going to tell you the basics so you can get started right now.

Crystals can have a seriously wonderful and positive impact on your life, and sometimes you can feel the benefits simply by holding the stone in your hand.

Put your crystal in your hand right now, take a deep breath, and notice how it feels. Does it feel warm or cold? Is it rough or smooth? Are there pointy edges? Does it feel heavy or light?

Simply be with the crystal for a short time—20 seconds—and see if you sense anything...extra. Be still. Be quiet. Maybe close your eyes. What did you feel?

Some people are really gifted with this kind of thing. We call those people *intuitive* or *empathic*. These are often the kind of people who just *know* when a friend could use a quick "How r u doing?" text. Intuitive or empathic people can sense the energy around them and know how to react.

Maybe you're not one of those people. I'm totally not! I have a hard time reading people, and I have an outrageously bad sense of timing. I'm the girl who makes the joke that no one thinks is funny. I'm the girl who just doesn't know what to say when a friend is hurting.

But I've learned to develop these gifts—the gifts

of intuition—and doing that has been a life-changing journey. And I learned a lot of my new skills from working with my crystals.

Okay, so perhaps you put the crystal in your hand, and—ZAP—you totally feel the energy. Great.

If you didn't, that's okay, too. Put it in your pocket and carry it around for the day. Or, if your first crystal is part of a piece of jewelry, just put it on and go about your day.

There's no need to force it. Just keep the energy of the crystal near your own energy field for a few hours and forget you've even got it with you.

At the end of the day, take a moment to think if anything was different. Were you a kinder person today? Did you feel calmer today than usual? Did you feel any magic? Make a mental note. Or write it out in your journal. If you're taking this journey with a friend, check in with them.

Sensing the energy might be hard for you. And, again, that's totally okay. Here's one thing that makes it even more complicated: Your energy may simply not work with a particular crystal. It's a problem I have from time to time.

The biggest example in my life is Emerald, a crystal that is associated with friendship and loyalty. (This is the same Emerald you probably know as a gemstone when it's cut and polished. But raw Emerald is duller, and it's got patchy green and black spots.) Holding an Emerald should inspire me to think of my friends and how lucky I am to have them. When I hold raw Emerald, I feel pretty terrible. One time I even had a bad memory flash in my mind, and I started to get really emotional.

I wanted to know why, so I asked my super cool friend Flora. She said that some crystals help to detox your body (you know, just like some people go on juice fasts) of old emotions and memories that you no longer need to hang on to. I had no idea this could happen, but I assume that is what happened when I held that Emerald that one time.

Flora also told me about a friend of hers who had a similar experience with Selenite, which also can be a detoxer. I've never had that problem with Selenite, though. Mostly, Selenite makes me feel light and happy and awesome. So different crystals work differently for different people, and that's why I've decided that, for the most part, Emerald and I do NOT get along. So I don't keep them around my house. And that's okay. Just like people, not everyone gets along all the time.

If you have an intense reaction to a crystal or notice that when you carry it around for a while you start to feel weird, that's all right. Maybe that crystal just doesn't "match" your energy very well. That's all right.

. . .

Your first crystal may be an Aquamarine, which the books tell you should make you feel like your soul is fresh and clean. Holding an Aquamarine may make you annoyed. Or sad. Or numb. If it does, drop it! It's not mixing well with your energy. Come back to it in a few weeks and see if anything changes. If not, flush it! Well, maybe give it to a friend.

You are a unique individual, and though one crystal may work for most people, it may not work for you. Again, that's totally okay.

(Don't literally flush a crystal down the toilet. You knew I was joking, right?)

CHAPTER 3
TAKING CARE OF YOUR CRYSTALS

Another thing you can try if a crystal is making you feel weird is to cleanse it. Just like people, crystals need regular cleaning, almost like giving your crystal a bath. As I already said, there are some crystals that you do not want to leave lying around in water or sunlight, as that can damage them. You don't want to neglect your lovely crystals! But you also don't want to let them go without cleansing, either.

Cleansing a crystal is also known as "charging" them. Yes, it does kinda sound like what you do with re-chargeable batteries. Just like people and batteries, crystals can get worn down over time. Especially if it's a crystal that detoxes, like Emerald, your crystal will need regular cleaning in order to keep doing its job. Since it goes around with you all day helping you feel positive and upbeat, it sometimes needs a little bath to wash off the angsty, dark feelings it might take on for you.

How will you know a crystal needs a little charge? Well, if it's normally a crystal that feels really good, but you notice after a few days or weeks of using it that it seems less powerful or gives you a strange feeling, you will know it needs a cleanse. This is easier to tell with practice, of course. People who are especially intuitive or empathic are really good at this.

Personally, I'm not very intuitive, so I just charge my crystals every time I am done using them, just in case. That way, I always know my crystals are squeaky clean and ready to go.

And how do you charge a crystal, you ask? Well, there are a few ways.

My favorite way to charge a crystal is to keep some Selenite in my crystal collection. Selenite is a crystal that charges other crystals! That's why it's awesome. If you want, you can also buy small bowls and plates made entirely of Selenite to place your crystals on. These are really nice, in my opinion, and they look pretty fancy. But a few small pieces of Selenite that you keep in your crystal drawer will do the trick. Selenite is also not very expensive, so you can get a few pieces easily and use them as crystals... and also to charge your other crystals.

If you don't have any Selenite, though, you can still give your crystals a little cleanse. You can run them under some cool water, then gently wipe them with a clean cloth. You don't need to rinse them for too long—a few seconds will do. Just make sure each side of the crystal touches the water. Think of it like brushing your teeth. You want to get every surface. Bonus points if you cleanse your crystals in natural water, like a nearby stream or creek. If you don't have one of those, though, the sink will do just fine!

You can also charge your crystals in sunlight or moonlight. Again, you don't want to leave your crystals lying in the sun for days—that will ruin them. I recommend placing your crystals in a sunny windowsill in the evening, then leaving them overnight so they can get some moonlight, then picking them up again in the morning before the sun gets too bright. That way they'll get a little sunlight and a little moonlight. That should do the trick.

If it helps you remember, you might choose to cleanse all your crystals once a month on the full moon. That way, you never forget to cleanse your crystals, and they get some super cool moon vibes to cleanse them regularly. You can set a reminder on your phone (if you have one) or ask an adult when the moon phases are and mark them on a calendar.

The moon is a really powerful way to connect with energy, as well, and it's also just really fun, in my opinion. Haley and I like to text each other at the full moon about our crystals and say we are charging them. It's not a big thing, it's just kinda nice.

One last way you can cleanse your crystals is bury them overnight, perhaps in a potted plant or on the edge of your yard. If you don't have access to any clean earth, you can also use a bowl of rice. Both of these work great, but you want to keep in mind that if you bury a crystal, it needs to be in a space that won't be in the way of anyone else and that you have permission to dig there. It can be a tiny hole, just enough to cover the crystals with dirt...but you need to be very, very careful that no one will mind that you dug up the dirt. Don't, for instance, bury them in your neighbor's flowerbed!

Crystals really value politeness, and they should never be used for harmful intent. They are only to be used to make the world a better place, so cleansing them in a way that leaves no trace is really important. If you don't have access to clean dirt, you can use a bowl of rice instead. Just make sure that in the morning, you rinse off the dirt (if you use the burying method) or throw away the rice (if you are using rice). Any rice you use will be filled with negative energies at this point, so you want to be sure not to eat it. Of course, you should only use rice that isn't going to be used in a recipe the very next day—make sure you have permission to throw the rice away when you're done, as well! Again, crystals are meant to be a positive force for good, so make sure your crystals are going to help people feel better, not become more trouble. It goes without saying that when you cleanse the crystals in the sink, you will clean up any water that gets on the floor. Crystals show us how to be kind, thoughtful people. They make the world a better place!

There are so many ways to cleanse crystals that I'm sure you will find one that works for you. In general, as long as you are cleansing your crystals every so often and keeping them out of direct sunlight, you are a great crystal caretaker. When I got my first crystals, it was only a few weeks before I was totally comfortable cleansing them. And they worked great!

I also try to keep any crystals I'm not using in a soft cloth bag. Most crystals you buy at a store or order online come in a soft cloth bag, anyway, which is a nice feature. This keeps the crystals from getting dinged up or chipped or broken. If you don't have any soft bags, though, a box or drawer will do just fine. I have a few boxes and bags in my house that are my go-to crystal hideaways. Haley has a gorgeous wooden jewelry box that was a present from her grandma, and she keeps her crystals in there. You probably already know just where to put your crystals. Anywhere they will be safe is a good spot.

All right, you are now an expert in how to take care of your crystals! I know they are in good hands. The next part of this book will teach you how to make the most of your crystal collection so they can start to work for you.

CHAPTER 4
SIMPLE CRYSTAL MEDITATION

The first thing you can try is a simple crystal meditation. Meditation is more and more common these days, and for a good reason! Research has shown that a few moments of quiet in your day can help you stay focused, in-the-moment, and less likely to make bad decisions.

Here's the simplest way to start a meditation practice. Set an alarm on your phone for a short time. Maybe three minutes. Get yourself into a comfortable position, like sitting with your legs crossed on a pillow. Or in a comfortable chair. I prefer to lie down. Rest the crystal on your body, on your forehead, in your lap, whatever feels right. Then start the countdown!

During the three minutes, your job is to do absolutely nothing except breathe. Concentrate on deep, cleansing breaths. If you find yourself thinking about homework or something someone said to you at school or what you plan to do later, try to let it go, just for the three minutes. You don't have to be mad at yourself for thinking these things, just gently move your attention back to your breath. You can always think about whatever you want as soon as the timer goes off.

Remember, everything is energy. Picture yourself in your room, in your house, in your town, on the planet. And feel everything around you. You can feel the air. You can feel the pillow. And you'll probably begin to feel... the crystal.

When the alarm sounds, take a mental note of what you experienced.

Meditation allows us to be exactly where we are. No stressing about the future. No regrets about the past. Just be present RIGHT NOW to what you feel. The more you meditate, the easier it gets, and the better you feel outside the time you are meditating, too.

People sometimes meditate with the help of a coach or with an app; it can be quite an elaborate affair. But it doesn't have to be. A quick crystal meditation is always available to you. Even if you only have time for one deep breath.

You can do this with any crystal to feel the energy it's providing you. Or you can pick and choose the energy you want! If you need to communicate with your mom, but you don't feel like you know what to say, choose a crystal for communication (a Blue Lace Agate or Lapis Lazuli) and do a quick meditation. You may be able to unlock the problems inside you and have the best conversation of your life.

Personally, every single morning I go to my collection of crystals and choose a few based on the challenges I'm probably going to face that day. I hold them for a moment, take a few deep breaths, and put a few in my pocket. That's a meditation! And it's been life-changing for me.

This practice has been revolutionary for me in my life. It's simple and effective. It's gotten me through some hard days. But I also do it on good days! I do it almost every day, but you can do it only once in a while, if you want. You will soon learn how often is right for you. And your crystals can help!

Like I said, we'll get into some more intricate ways to use crystals later in the book, but meditation is the basis for all of it. So practicing this, even one deep breath at a time, will really help you become more intuitive.

· · ·

It's simple. But it's not easy. Keep at it! And after a while, you'll be able to pick up any crystal and immediately feel what it can offer you at that moment.

CHAPTER 5

ADDING CRYSTALS TO YOUR COLLECTION

Okay, when you have one crystal, you're in the game.

When you have two or more, you've got a COLLECTION! How exciting!

Now how do you decide which precious crystal treasures you should get?

As I mentioned, the best way to find new crystals is to use your intuition. But if that isn't quite working for you yet, you can always look them up. Use this book as a reference, or use Google. Type in something like:

"Crystals for feeling tired"
"What crystal helps you study?"
"Crystal meaning Violet Fluorite"

And just see what comes up. If you see a crystal that looks interesting to you, either because of its shape or color or what the Internet says it can do for you, that means it's a good crystal for you to try. If it's in your budget, buy it the next time you see one! Or add it to your wish list for when you grow your collection.

The rest of this section will help you explore some ways of choosing crystals. As you go through, see which crystals "jump out" at you. If they seem interesting to you, they are probably good crystals for you to try.

ZODIAC CRYSTALS

If you want to, you can also choose a crystal based on your birthday.

One of the many ways people try to understand the mysteries of the universe is to look to the skies. Not just astrology—you know, like what's your Zodiac sign?—but also the history and folklore about the planets and the stars. The stars and planets that were prominent in the sky when you were born actually have some influence in your life —everything is energy, remember? So whatever was going on in the sky when you were born marks a few things about you, more or less. It's not a hard and fast rule, more like a guideline. Let me show you what I mean.

For example, I'm a Leo. Leo is the Latin word for "lion," so people born under this sign are bold, assertive people, just like the king of the jungle, the lion! Because I'm a Leo, I've always been that girl who has great ideas and loves to share them with others. Then we make them happen! It's lots of fun.

Being a Leo also means that sometimes I get a bit ahead of myself, jumping to conclusions and taking charge even when it's not my turn to speak up.

I love being a Leo, but before I became a crystal girl, I didn't always know how to show leadership in ways that were good for me—or everyone else. Now that I've learned to like myself just the way I am, being a Leo is tons of fun! And crystals have been a big part of that for me.

Haley is a Libra. That means she's a peacemaker. She is so good at making friends and comforting people when they are feeling down. She's a great listener and always makes people feel welcome.

I adore Haley, obviously, and think she's one of the nicest people I know—of course, I'm a little biased! But Haley shared with me (and she says it's okay to share this with you, too) that sometimes being a Libra is hard for her. Since she's the one everyone goes to with their problems, she sometimes isn't as comfortable sharing her own with them when it's her turn. This is part of the reason Rose Quartz is such a good crystal for her, I think. It helps her see that there is enough love in the world for *everyone*—including her.

This part of the book will help you choose a crystal based on your astrological sign, if you want. It's a great place to get started, and it might also help you like yourself, just the way you are. Part of being a crystal girl/guy is knowing that everyone is great, already, without trying, no matter what. We are all our own person and have lots to offer the world.

So without further ado, here is a list of the astrological signs, and a crystal associated with each.

Aries (March 21-April 19)

Carnelian

People born under the sign of Aries are known to be strong-willed when they want something. You can't stop them. But many Aries folks struggle with doubt. Carnelian will light that fire, give you confidence, and let you knock down any walls ahead of you.

Taurus (April 20-May 20)

Smoky Quartz

Taurus folks are often people really skilled at slow and steady growth—that is when they are calm and focused. When it's hard to find that focus, Smoky Quartz makes you feel supported and strong so you can keep getting better.

Gemini (May 21-June 20)

Shungite

Gemini is the sign of the twins. So most Geminis can often have really strong and conflicting opinions. Shungite can help you find the right way when there are too many good (or bad) choices.

Cancer (June 21-July 22)
Labradorite

Cancers are really loving and protective people. The beauty of Labradorite is that it reminds Cancers to take care of themselves, too.

Leo (July 23-August 22)
Tiger's Eye

Leos tend to be natural leaders. That's a lot of pressure! Sometimes a Leo needs some support and power from the crystal that pumps you up and keeps you energized— Tiger's Eye!

Virgo (August 23-September 22)
Amazonite

If you need help, find a Virgo. It's what they do! Amazonite is a great complement because it is really soothing and balancing. It'll enhance the gifts a Virgo already has.

Libra (September 23-October 22)
Bloodstone

People born under the sign of Libra are often wise. They're the people you go to when you need advice. A Libra with a Bloodstone (the stone of wisdom) will give you the best advice you've ever heard.

Scorpio (October 23-November 21)
Citrine

Citrine is a stone that helps you make goals and finish what you start. In fact, it's a pleasure to get to work with a Citrine in your pocket. This is a perfect match for a Scorpio because they dream big!

Sagittarius (November 22-December 21)
Lepidolite

"Life is one long journey of discovery" is the kind of thing a Sagittarius would say. And holding Lepidolite is like holding a universe of possibilities in your hand. Perfect match for a Sag!

Capricorn (December 22-January 19)
Rose Quartz

A Capricorn rarely asks for a "thank you." They just like to help. But that can wear on a person. The antidote is Rose Quartz, which reminds you that you can give and receive love without limit!

. . .

Aquarius (January 20-February 18)

Sodalite

If you need a creative solution to a problem, find an Aquarian! They always think outside of the box. But sometimes, they tend to dream too much. Put a piece of Sodalite in their hand, and its calm, rational energy will give them good balance.

Pisces (February 19-March 20)

Clear Quartz

A Pieces will always be there to help you—to give you support, advice, and care. Clear Quartz helps things heal. So a Pisces with the master healing crystal? Unstoppable!

BIRTHSTONES

You also are probably familiar with your birthstone. Sometimes moms will wear a ring or a necklace with the birthstones of each of her kids. That's the gemstone assigned to the month in which each of her kids was born.

The idea of birthstones can be traced back 2000 years, but the modern list of birthstones... well... it was pretty much made up by people who sell jewelry. So these connections are not as powerful. But a gem is a crystal, so maybe your birthstone will connect you the exact energy you need.

January

Garnet

Garnet is fiery! It's got the energy of a roaring fire. Wild, free and exciting.

February

Amethyst

If things are hectic, pick up an Amethyst, and the calming energy will bring you back down.

March

Aquamarine

"Go with the flow!" That's what an Aquamarine will try to teach you. Calm yourself down and trust the universe.

April

Diamond

Diamonds are as close to perfect as a stone gets. And holding diamonds will make you feel indestructible!

May

Emerald

Friendship! An Emerald can be your friend when you need one and remind you to be a good friend to others at the same time.

June

Pearl

If you need some good luck, a Pearl will help you move in the right direction. It's also got the calming energy of flowing water.

July

Ruby

If you need to come up with an idea for a school

project, or for a great birthday present, Ruby will help you be creative and motivated.

August
Peridot

Green for good luck—you get that from a Peridot. But it also keeps you from getting caught up in the drama around you.

September
Sapphire

Sapphires are the best gem to put in a crown. They are the crystals of royalty. They remind you that you are important, and that people should respect you.

October
Opal

If you're feeling gloomy, and you need some optimism in your life, grab an Opal, look at its gorgeous shine, and be reminded that things will turn out okay.

November
Topaz

If you are mad at your brother or sister and can't seem to get over it, a Topaz will help you find forgiveness in your heart.

December

Turquoise

This gem is like wearing armor! If you've got a Turquoise in your hand, no one can hurt you.

CHAKRA SETS

This may be a little advanced, but I think you can handle it. If you look for crystals online, you may find what are known as "chakra sets." These are a set of (usually) seven crystals that represent the whole rainbow of colors that you'll find in crystals.

Before we talk about what "chakras" are (usually pronounced "shock-ruh" or "chock-ruh"), we have to take a detour and talk about color.

Have you ever heard someone say that they can read "auras"? The same way that some people can pick up a crystal and know exactly what kind of energy it has, some people can look at living things (people, trees, dogs) and sense that energy immediately. And these people often describe that energy with colors.

"Your aura is very dark gray today. Are you feeling okay?"
"I knew you were going to win the spelling bee—your aura was glowing orange!"

Certain kinds of energy have certain colors. And they're not random. And this goes for the colors of crystals, too.

Think of the color red, for example. The first

thing you'll probably think of is fire! Red crystals tend to have a fiery energy to them. They help you get inspired and keep going even when you're tired.

How about blue? When you think of blue, what do you think of? The ocean, maybe? Blue crystals tend to help us feel calm, like we're staring out into the vastness of the ocean.

So yeah, energy has color! And the more you work with crystals, or other practices like it, you'll start to see them yourself. It's not always easy—even for me, who has been practicing for years—but when you catch a glimpse of a purple light coming from someone you love, you'll know they are confident and grateful. It can be really exciting to see the world this way.

Okay, now back to chakras!

I mentioned earlier that all people are made of energy. And as we've learned, energy flows and changes and slows down/speeds up—it's constantly moving through your body.

The culture of India teaches us that energy flow isn't all random; there is some order to it! This philosophy tells us that we have energy centers called "chakras" that run up and down our bodies. There are hundreds of these chakras in a person, but there seem to be seven main ones.

Each of the seven chakras has a location in the

body, and it has a kind of energy that it keeps organized. And, yes, each one has a color!

Let me tell you about each chakra, and you'll see what I mean.

1—The Root Chakra

    Location: The base of your spine

    Color: Black, red, and brown

    Energy: Staying grounded

If you ever feel like you are off-balance in your life—if things are out of control—that means you're not feeling grounded. Concentrating your meditation on your root chakra, with some added help from a root chakra crystal, will help you feel more in control.

Root Chakra Crystals:

    Hematite

    Red Jasper

    Obsidian

2—The Sacral Chakra

Location: Just behind your belly button

Color: Orange

Energy: Creativity, joy, play

If you're feeling sad or uninspired, you probably have something blocking your sacral chakra from letting energy flow through it. Think about the area behind your belly button, and breathe into it. Use a crystal to help. You can even rest the crystal on your belly while you breathe. Working on this chakra will help remind you that there is joy and fun in the world.

Sacral Chakra Crystals:

Carnelian

Citrine

Honey Calcite

3—The Solar Plexus Chakra

Location: Below your ribcage

Color: Yellow, gold, amber

Energy: Personal power, intelligence, ambition

I like to the think of the solar plexus chakra as where the Superman symbol would be if I was wearing the costume. We just instinctually know that when you feel powerful, it comes from that part of your body. So when you don't feel like people are paying attention to you, or you feel scared to do something, concentrate on this part of your body. Maybe throw in a yellow crystal.

Solar Plexus Chakra Crystals:

Pyrite

Tiger's Eye

Amber

4—The Heart Chakra

Location: In your heart!

Color: Pink and Green

Energy: Love, compassion, emotional balance

This chakra is probably the easiest to identify. If you've ever been on love or had a heartbreak, you know that feeling centers in your chest—in your heart. Concentrating on that part of your body can help! And if you have a heart chakra crystal necklace, let it sit right by your heart, so it can do some work for you.

Heart Chakra Crystals:

Rose Quartz

Malachite

Jade

5—The Throat Chakra

Location: Your throat

Color: Blue

Energy: Communication, self-expression

Did you ever hear someone say that an idea was stuck in their throat? When we can't communicate well, we feel tension right there. This is the throat chakra being clogged with negative energy. Get it out! Meditate while thinking about your throat. And add a blue crystal into the mix to help it out.

Throat Chakra Crystals:

Blue Lace Agate

Amazonite

Blue Kyanite

6—The Third Eye Chakra
Location: Just above the center of your eyebrows
Color: Purple
Energy: Intuition/spiritual gifts, psychic powers

Do you ever see ghosts? Do you ever feel like you have the power to predict what someone is going to say or do? We all have some special gifts that are mysterious. If you want to sharpen those gifts, grab a purple crystal and hold it to your third eye chakra. We are all powerful beings, but we do have to work on our gifts.

Third Eye Chakra Crystals:
Amethyst
Lepidolite
Lapis Lazuli

7—The Crown Chakra
Location: Right at the very top of your head
Color: Purple, clear, and white
Energy: Connection to everything, harmony

This is probably my favorite chakra. When you feel lonely, or like people don't take you seriously, you are having problems with your crown chakra. Remember we are all energy. EVERYTHING IS ENERGY, and we stay connected to it through our crown. Working on this chakra will help you understand that you're special, and the universe knows it.

Crown Chakra Crystals:
Clear Quartz
Selenite
Howlite

CHAPTER 6

GETTING SOME OF
THAT CRYSTAL MAGIC!

If you are still unsure about which crystals are right for you, you can look through these scenarios and see which ones jump out at you right now. Of course, you can still choose crystals based on a certain chakra you want to work on or in honor of your birthstone, but there are lots of other crystals you can choose from, too.

On a more day-to-day basis, try using these particular crystals to support you when times get a little tough. Since crystals are meant to help us through tricky situations, hopefully this list will help you in finding the right crystal for whatever you are going through at the moment (or in the future).

These are mine and Haley's go-to crystals for when we're going through a rough time, but that doesn't mean you can't get lots of great benefits from lots of other crystals, too. If you already use different crystals for these same situations, that's totally fine. Whatever crystal you are drawn to is the right crystal for you, after all. Still, here are some ideas to spark your creativity, especially as when life gets stressful, we aren't always as in tune with our intuition. I know I have my must-have crystals for certain situations—for instance, I will never leave home without my Tiger's Eye if I have a big presentation at work.

Taking a Test

Azurite is a powerful stone for insight and wisdom and will really help you when studying for tests. It will also be great to take into the test with you, either to keep in your pocket or set on your desk if you are allowed. If you look at the Azurite while studying and then keep it near you while taking the test, you are more likely to remember everything you learned!

Another great stone for taking tests is Black Tourmaline, as it's very calming and can help with pre-test jitters. Keeping Black Tourmaline near you while you take your exam can help you stay grounded. After all, if you *believe* you know the right answers, you are more likely to answer correctly, even if you think you are just guessing!

Giving a Presentation

When I have to give a presentation at work, I always take a Tiger's Eye along, either in my pocket or as a necklace. Tiger's Eye is wonderful for boosting confidence and helping you feel like what you have to say is important.

You can also use Blue Kyanite, which is a great stone for confidence and speaking. Haley likes Blue Kyanite for when she sings—she's a great singer but doesn't always believe she is. Having a Blue Kyanite with her when she performs is really supportive.

Sports and Athletics

If you are an athlete, you might take Sodalite with you in your sports bag to help you focus. Of course, you probably can't take the stone with you onto the playing field or out on the track, but just knowing it is in your bag might be all the support you need.

Amethyst is another good stone for athletes, as it can help you visualize yourself scoring the winning point, then believing in your ability to do it. Amethyst is a great crystal for believing in yourself.

Arts, Music, and Other Hobbies

If you love music, art, theater, dance, or other creative hobbies, you might benefit from using Carnelian, a powerful stone of creation. Carnelian is a bright, fiery gemstone sure to inspire you in whatever art you pursue.

You might also enjoy using Clear Quartz, a great stone for mental clarity and focus. Clear Quartz magnifies any energies you have within you, and it also magnifies other stones it is near, so it's a great booster for the innate talents you've got inside you, just waiting to get out!

Arguments and Hurt Feelings

Sometimes it's hard to get along with others in our family or our group of friends, of course. We all do our best, but everyone gets their feelings hurt from time to time! For those times, I recommend Rose Quartz. Seriously. It always makes me feel so much better, and we've already talked about what a powerful source of love it can be.

You might also try Moonstone after a disagreement. It comes in several varieties (including Green, Blue, Pink, and Rainbow!), so look for the color that suits you best. It's a very calming, peaceful stone, and you might want to wear it near your heart for the days when you need some strength to be calm and peaceful even when others are not.

Friendships and Relationships

When you are hoping someone is going to be your friend—or maybe more than a friend!—you might need a little added courage to support you in feeling calm when you hang out with them. For these times, I like to carry Malachite. It's a supportive stone for loyalty, courage, and balance. It's also good for keeping negative feelings and thoughts at bay, and I like to wear it as a necklace so it's close to my heart.

Another good stone for friendships and relationships is Jade. Jade is good for love and trust and support, and it's also really lucky. It also supports peace, harmony, and balance. Carrying a Jade stone for luck when you hang out with someone new is always a safe bet.

• • •

Luck, Money, and Finding a New Job

Whether you have a job, get an allowance, or just help around the house, we all like to have a little luck now and then! Crystals can serve as a "lucky" charm to help focus our attention on all the blessings around us, whether it's money, or friendship, or the presents we get on our birthday, whatever. I like to use Citrine to help me focus on luck and prosperity.

Pyrite is another great stone for luck and money. It's often called "fool's gold," because it kinda looks like real gold, even though it isn't actually gold. Still, it's such a sparkly, fun stone that I just love to have it around!

Health Concerns, Grief, and Loss

I know firsthand how hard it can be if someone you love, or even you yourself are dealing with serious health issues. It's scary and stressful to think that someone you care about isn't feeling their best and might not be able to spend time with you in the way that they used to. For this, I like to use Bloodstone. It's a supportive, emotionally healing gemstone that's really good for dealing with fear and loss.

Bloodstone is one of those stones that can cause an emotional detox, so if you are already feeling upset, it's okay to hang on to a Bloodstone for a little while and let those emotions out. This can be really supportive on tough days after something difficult happens.

Another good stone for this is Black Onyx. It's a very grounding stone, and it also reminds you that you are a warrior who can handle anything! On days when you still need to go to school and function as a normal human being even when someone in your life is struggling, Black Onyx is great for courage and strength, even if it's hard.

Mental and Emotional Health

I could spend all day talking about the crystals I use for my own anxiety! Still, here are two you can use: Hematite and Lava Stone. Hematite is a grounding, calming stone that's wonderful at clearing away jitters, whether it's social anxiety, night terrors, or just general anxiety that won't go away, no matter what you do. Hematite won't replace any medication you take or make your anxiety go away permanently, but it can help you feel much more relaxed and calm if you hold some Hematite in your hand whenever you are feeling particularly anxious.

Another stone I really like for anxiety is Lava Stone. It is literally cooled lava, straight from a volcano. It's super light and filled with holes. If you or anyone in your house likes to use essential oils, you can actually place some calming essential oils (such as lavender or peppermint) on the Lava Stone. The Lava Stone will smell nice all day and help you feel calmer, too. I have a Lava Stone bracelet that I use for this, and I almost never leave home without it!

CHAPTER 7
OTHER WAYS TO USE CRYSTALS

All right, so you probably have a few crystals by now. And you've mastered all the tips and tricks for meditating with them, taking care of them, and using them on a daily basis. But there are lots of more "advanced" ways to use crystals, and once you start to get really good at the basics, it's always fun to level up.

Even if these techniques seem "advanced," I started learning them after being a crystal girl for only a few weeks. I'm sure you can handle them, no problem.

Making Your Own Jewelry

Have you ever made your own jewelry? Well, now you can make your own healing jewelry! Since you've learned all about the properties of various crystals, now when you make jewelry, you can buy beads made from various healing stones. The other materials can be ordinary wire or hemp cord or whatever you usually use; the only "new" ingredient is crystals.

Sometimes ordinary craft stores have real crystal beads, or you can ask at your local crystal shop. You can also order them online. Maybe you and your friends can get together and make healing crystal jewelry. Haley did this once for her birthday party. She invited me to see the jewelry when it was done, and it turned out amazing!

The nice thing about making your own jewelry is it is very customizable, so you can match your own vibe. Whether you are more feminine, more masculine, something in between, or something else altogether, you can definitely find jewelry that suits you if you switch it up and make it yourself! If you are sensitive to certain jewelry components (such as nickel-plated metal), you can also make sure your custom jewelry meets all your needs.

Mixing and matching different types of crystals

can be really powerful here, and you will know which combos to use for your specific needs. Maybe you are a sports-musician-artsy person and you need a crystal combination that supports you in all three. Or maybe you are both an outdoorsy and indoorsy person, and you need something that balances the two sides of your nature. Whatever your vibe, you can definitely find the right crystals to support it.

Crystal Grids

Speaking of combinations, if you ever feel like you want to combine the energies of a few different crystals, crystal grids are the way to go! A crystal "grid" is just a fancy arrangement for your crystals, all laid out in a pattern. You can download and print crystal grid patterns from the Internet, or you can simply arrange them in any way that feels good to you.

The nice thing about crystal grids is that you can use them to combine the energies of various crystals and help them work together. This helps them be even more powerful, as does the geometric patterns you arrange them in.

So maybe you want to combine the power of lepidolite, rose quartz, Howlite, and selenite so you can get a good night's rest the night before an important test or the big game. All you do is take a few of each crystal and arrange them in a pattern using straight lines, circles, and other geometric arrangements. The straighter and neater the arrangement, the more powerful, but you can set them in any pattern that feels right to you. That's why downloading a grid guide can be helpful, but it's definitely not a necessity. Just arrange the crystals in whatever way looks good and feels good to you.

Set an intention for your grid and then step back and let it do the work. Maybe the intention is, "I want to sleep better tonight," or "I want to do well on my test tomorrow." Whatever your intention, the crystals will know what to do! By arranging them with this specific intention and choosing the crystals to match, the grid will be able to do its work.

Grids get "tired," just like individual crystals (and just like people), so you don't want to leave a grid set up for longer than a few days. After a day or two, you can take it apart and put it back together again, this time with different crystals, a different pattern, or both. Your needs will change over the course of a few days anyway, so resetting your grids often will help both you and the crystals get the support you need.

. . .

Crystal Bags

What if you want the power of a crystal grid but in a handy portable format? Crystal bags are the answer. Basically, it's just a crystal grid, but you put the mix of crystals you want in a small cloth bag (the kind that crystals come wrapped in when you buy them work really well for this). Then you carry that bag with you throughout the day: in your pocket, in your backpack, in your purse, wherever.

Once you get good at this, you can start to create your own "recipes" for crystal bags for special occasions or whenever you need them. Maybe you want to incorporate some crystals for friendship and money, or the root chakra and anxiety. Or another combination altogether. You will know which stones you want to put in, and they will all work together nicely once you do.

Sometimes I put some of the stones I need the most in a bag and place it under my pillow before I go to sleep. I usually sleep better, have better dreams, and whatever purpose I set for the stones is much more likely to come true.

Crystal bags are lots of fun! They're so satisfying to feel that small lump with me wherever I go. After about a day, the crystals will need a recharge, so be sure to take them out and cleanse them in the usual way. Then you can always put them back in the same bag together or mix and match into a new bag. You will know what seems right for you—just go with your gut and see what great combinations you come up with.

CHAPTER 8
49 OF MY FAVORITE CRYSTALS

Below is a list of every single crystal I've mentioned in the book so far—listed alphabetically—plus a few more of my super-favorites. Use this as a guide when you're choosing, or look up the crystals you already have for ideas!

Amazonite

Color: Light to medium green, ranges from yellow-green to teal

Chakra: Heart

Zodiac: Virgo

Amazonite is a balancing, harmonizing stone that helps you get all your energy centers into alignment. It's great for creativity and positivity, as well as helping you feel all around happier.

With Amazonite around, you feel calmer, stronger, and more aligned. You can tackle big projects or handle big emotions because you're so at one with everything! Extra helpful for speaking up and speaking out, and even tackling arguments and disagreements.

Try this: Wear Amazonite on a day when you need a little extra courage to speak up for what you know is right. It makes great bracelets and necklaces, or you can keep it in your pocket instead.

Amber

Color: Dark yellow-gold, amber-colored
Chakra: Solar plexus
Zodiac: n/a

Have you ever seen small babies wearing an amber necklace? It's for when their gums hurt when they're teething. Amber is really helpful for aches and pains. Amber is also beneficial for making good choices and being true to yourself.

Try this: Wear an Amber bracelet if you have aches and pains after a workout. Carry Amber in your pocket for courage on days when you need a reminder of who you really are.

Amethyst
> Color: Purple with white veins
> Chakra: Third Eye/Crown
> Zodiac: n/a

Amethyst is good for intuition, wisdom, and insight. It's also good for developing psychic gifts and brighter dreams. It's also a really good stone for calming the mind and soothing emotions.

So if you want clearer thoughts and a higher perspective, keep Amethyst near to awaken your inner sight.

Try this: Put an Amethyst under your pillow or by your bed for clearer, kinder dreams and better sleep at night. You can also wear it as a pendant or a bracelet for better mental health throughout your day.

Aquamarine

Color: Aqua, light blue-green

Chakra: Throat

Zodiac: n/a

Aquamarine is an expressive, bright stone that's really good for helping you live and speak your truth. It's named after the calming, cleansing power of the ocean, as its name literally comes from the color of the sea. If you want to feel calm, respectful, and powerful, look no further than Aquamarine—because that's how the ocean tends to be, too!

Try this: Wear or carry Aquamarine on days when you need to channel your inner mermaid/merman/merperson or just want to feel like you are walking along the beach.

Azurite

    Color: Deep blue, with flecks of green
    Chakra: Throat, third eye
    Zodiac: Sagittarius

Azurite is a deep blue stone with a sparkly sheen, and it's very good for setting intentions and opening up your awareness to the unknown. Any intuition and insight you need, Azurite has your back. It's also really good for speaking and living your truth, as its deep blue color resonates with the throat chakra.

Try this: Include some Azurite in a crystal grid for calming your mind and focusing your thoughts, and then expressing them clearly.

Black Onyx

Color: Black with a shiny metallic sheen, some-times marbled with traces of white

Chakra: Root

Zodiac: n/a

Black Onyx is just the darkest colored variety of onyx, but boy, is it strong! It's a deeply grounding stone with powerful protection abilities, so wear it to keep negative people and situations out of your life.

This stone is also good for helping you with what's called your "shadow side," which is all the ways that your weaknesses or stuff that has happened to you weigh you down. Part of being a human is learning to understand and accept these parts of ourselves, but then release them so we can rise above our challenges. Black Onyx can help you do this, as it always gives you strength to overcome.

Try this: Wear or carry Black Onyx on a day when you will need lots of strength to overcome chal-lenges and steer clear of negativity in your life.

Black Tourmaline

Color: Black, with a rough vertical surface

Chakra: Root

Zodiac: n/a

Black Tourmaline is my go-to for protection against annoying or negative situations, or really just any time I know I will be stressed or overstimulated. It's great for keeping you calm and grounded, no matter what tries to pull you off your center. That's why it's such a great stone for mental health.

This is a really popular and powerful stone, and you can use it to keep away anything negative in your life. It's almost like an amulet of protection, and you can literally place it between you and negative people, toxic situations, or anything else you don't want too much of in your life.

Try this: Pair a Black Tourmaline stone with a Rose Quartz stone in a bracelet or necklace, and wear it on a day when you need to be in a large crowd or deal with a lot of noise. You can also take a large piece of Black Tourmaline and set it between you and someone else who's really negative or complains all the time, and you can put it between you and any dark parts in your house (such as between you and your closet at night).

Bloodstone

Color: Green, usually with small red flecks

Chakra: Heart

Zodiac: Aries

Bloodstone is good for emotional healing, and it's really powerful for the heart chakra. Use this stone any time you have some intense emotions you want to release, such as a time when you think it might feel nice to cry but you're too stressed to let any tears out.

This is a good stone for courage and creativity, also, and just being free to express yourself and your emotions freely.

Try this: Hold on to a Bloodstone for a few minutes and see what emotions come up for you. If you feel called to laugh, or cry, or express yourself in some way, just do it. Let the stone bring out whatever needs to be released.

Blue Lace Agate

Color: Icy blue streaked with white (sometimes tan/brown on the edges)

Chakra: Throat

Zodiac: Gemini, Pisces

If you hold a Blue Lace Agate up to the light, you'll see why it got its name—it's full of filmy, frosty swirls of light blue and white, and it's so pretty! It often comes in very thin slices so you can see the colors especially well. Blue Lace Agate is good for speaking your truth, and it's also calming and balancing. You can use it for courage and clear communication, as well as honesty and strength.

Try this: Wear a Blue Lace Agate as a necklace to support you in truthful speaking.

Calcite (general)

Color: Black, white, blue, gray, green, orange, red, or clear

Chakra: Based on the color

Zodiac: Cancer

Calcite comes in a variety of colors, so choose the one(s) that feel best to you! In general, the color will affect how it makes you feel, so pay attention to what you're drawn to and go from there. Most Calcite stones, though, are really uplifting and supportive, so they will make you feel cheerful and happy. They're good for a positive attitude and combatting dark or depressive thoughts, so carry one whenever you want to feel just a little more encouraged.

They're also really good stones to give as gifts for this reason; you can choose a Calcite based on your friend or family member's favorite color, then give it to them so they feel positive and relaxed.

Try this: Give Calcite as a gift or keep one in your pocket on a day when you need just a little more encouragement.

Carnelian

Color: Deep red or orange

Chakra: Sacral, root

Zodiac: Virgo

Carnelian is a powerful, bright stone that uplifts the mood and boosts creativity and strength. Keeping Carnelian nearby when you do art, music, exercise, math, or anything else that requires your full attention is a great idea. In fact, you probably don't want to keep it by your bed, it's so energizing! It's great for memory, focus, and digging in and getting stuff done. I have also used it to help with symptoms of PMS, if that's something you have.

Try this: Keep Carnelian near your workspace or in your pocket to energize you when getting work done, especially creative work.

Celestite

Color: Whitish, clear, and tinted with blue, gray, yellow, green, or brown

Chakra: Third eye, crown

Zodiac: n/a

Celestite is named after the heavens, and it's clear why! Celestite looks like ice crystals, and it's a powerful stone of connection to the heavens and higher realms. For this reason, it's very calming. It helps you find your inner Zen guru, so using Celestite to meditate is always a plus. It's also good for mindfulness, mental health, and good sleep.

Try this: Meditate with Celestite right before bed to open you up to peaceful dreams and a light, calm feeling before you go to sleep.

Citrine
    Color: Clear golden yellow
    Chakra: Solar plexus
    Zodiac: n/a

Citrine is a great stone for wealth and abundance, so use Citrine when you need to focus on getting a new job or getting good grades. It also helps with self-esteem, self-image, and focusing your intentions. It also amplifies whatever energies you're already focusing on, so it's a good thing that it's also an uplifting and positive stone! Use Citrine any time you need to power through with positivity.

Try this: Include Citrine in a grid for wishing for a specific gift or goal (such as more money or more friends or that new pair of shoes you *really* want for your birthday). Then go out and do everything in your power to make your dream(s) a reality! The Universe helps out when you put in the effort, so do extra chores or odd jobs in your neighborhood whenever you can to help the Universe out.

Clear Quartz
Color: Clear
Chakra: Crown
Zodiac: n/a

Clear Quartz is a glassy clear stone that actually amplifies the power of every other stone, so it's useful for whatever you want it for! It's also a good protection stone, though, especially at night. It cleanses and purifies negativity and supports whatever intentions you set it for. Clear Quartz can also help with mental "clutter," for clear thoughts and better mental health. It's an all-around workhorse, so you will want to add it to your collection if you can.

Try this: Use Clear Quartz next to your other crystals to amplify their abilities, perhaps in a grid, in a bag, or just under your pillow or in your pocket.

Diamond
> Color: Clear (might be tinted)
> Chakra: All
> Zodiac: n/a

Lots of the diamond jewelry you buy is made of synthetic material, but the real thing is actually a powerful healing stone. Diamonds are useful for focusing on new projects and mental clarity. That's why it's so good for keeping a calm mind and boosting your ability to sleep. That's also why Diamonds are great for meditation—they help you stay clear and focused, free from distractions. Even a small diamond can make a big difference, so don't discredit that small diamond ring you found in a thrift store. It might be that the diamond wants to help you with clear focus!

Try this: Wear diamond jewelry to help with meditation or any time you need to focus on something for a long time (such as when taking a test).

Emerald (raw and gemstone)

Color: Green
Chakra: Heart
Zodiac: Taurus

Emeralds are powerful, either in their raw, uncut form or once they've been shaped into glittering gemstones. Emerald jewelry or rough stones are both wonderful for balancing emotions, supporting patience, friendship, and forgiveness, and releasing emotions trapped in your body as trauma. It's great for experiencing unconditional love and compassion for the planet and everyone on it.

Try this: Wear an Emerald necklace near your heart chakra or carry one in your pocket to help you have more love for everyone around you, perhaps when helping out at a local charity or when people at work or school are hard to get along with.

Garnet
    Color: Deep red or burgundy
    Chakra: Heart, root
    Zodiac: Aquarius

Garnet is wonderful for balance in times of transition or change. They keep the emotions balanced so we can stay stable, even if things feel a bit chaotic or unsettled. It can help you stay strong when things are rough or strange.

It's also a great stone for friendship, enthusiasm, and creativity.

Try this: Carry or wear garnet whenever you are going through a rocky patch in life, perhaps changing schools, moving to a new house, or if anything else feels unsettled or chaotic.

Green Aventurine

    Color: Green with dark specks

    Chakra: Heart

    Zodiac: n/a

Aventurine is a great stone for leadership and emotional healing, especially Green Aventurine, which is often the type you find in your favorite shops. Green Aventurine, especially, is amazing for balancing and soothing emotions. It's a healer of the heart and works well with the heart chakra. So it's great for inner harmony and balance, especially between the heart and mind.

Try this: Keep a Green Aventurine in your yoga bag so you will have it near when you go to yoga class. It'll help you balance your mind, body, and heart. If you don't do yoga, you can always take it on a walk or whenever you are called to be a leader among your friends or family.

Hematite

Color: Dark silvery gray with a shiny sheen

Chakra: Root

Zodiac: n/a

Hematite is a highly grounding stone to help you feel centered and powerful. It also is good for clear thoughts, so feel free to take one with you to a math test! Hematite is a good protection stone, too.

In fact, Hematite is a great all-around stone to have in your crystal arsenal, and it works great as jewelry or just by itself. It's often found in gift shops, so if you're ever on vacation, keep an eye out for some Hematite. It makes an excellent worry stone to keep you feeling calm and supported even when you're stressed out from traveling so much.

Try this: Keep a couple pieces of Hematite in your pocket and pull them out whenever you're stressed. They make great fidgets to play with when you need something to help you calm down.

Honey Calcite

Color: Honey-colored yellow or gold
Chakra: Solar plexus
Zodiac: n/a

Honey Calcite is a happy, positive stone sure to help you feel light and upbeat. It's great for confidence and self-assurance, so use it any time you need to make a big decision or stick with a decision you've already made. Or both!

Honey Calcite is also really good for self-esteem and self-efficacy, so it can be great support when you need to do something hard, like overcome a challenge. You can keep a Honey Calcite nearby and tell yourself, "I bring positive change to the world." Then go out and make it happen.

Try this: Keep a Honey Calcite near you whenever you need to make a difficult decision, accomplish a hard task, or overcome a challenge. It will keep you feeling strong, confident, and courageous.

Howlite

Color: Milky white with gray or black veins

Chakra: Third eye

Zodiac: n/a

Howlite is the stone of rest and relaxation. It allows you to slow your brain, live in the moment, and experience the gratitude that's hard to capture sometimes. It's also associated with self-healing—physical, emotional, and spiritual.

You can use it during the day when you feel like you're being a hothead. And use it at night to give your whole being the rest it deserves. You'll heal physically, emotionally, and spiritually.

Try this: Put a big hunk of Howlite under your bed, directly below your pillow. If you're having trouble sleeping, rely on Howlite to calm your brain, slow down your heartbeat, and get the rest and healing you desperately need.

Jade

Color: Bright green (can also be white, black, gray, or blue)

Chakra: Heart

Zodiac: n/a

Jade has been famous for centuries as a stone of protection and harmony. So if you want your loved one to feel safe on a long trip, give them some jade before they leave! It will help them focus on feeling secure. It's also a good stone for trustworthiness, joyfulness, and love. Jade is very common in jewelry, so you can find it all over.

Try this: Wear some jade on a long trip or give it as a gift for someone who will be away for a long time. Or wear it any time you want to feel safe, secure, and connected to someone important to you.

Jasper (General)

Color: All colors—usually multi-colored
Chakra: All (based on color)
Zodiac: n/a

Jasper is a wonderfully versatile stone with a variety of uses. Depending on its color, it can help with all kinds of things. Overall, Jasper is good for balancing intense emotions, such as anger or fear or even extreme joy. When you want to feel chilled out and balanced, Jasper is your friend. All the amazing colors, too, are just kinda exciting to look at. It's hard to look at a Jasper stone and feel sad!

Try this: Notice which color of Jasper you are most drawn to. This is probably the chakra in most need of some help right now. Keep that Jasper in your pocket and notice how it makes you feel.

Kyanite (General) / Blue Kyanite

Color: Black, gray, white, green, yellow, or pink/blue

Chakra: All/throat

Zodiac: n/a

Kyanite is a popular stone, but Blue Kyanite is the most popular. Blue Kyanite is usually used for speaking clearly and authentically, as well as standing up for what you know is right.

It's also really good for working through disagreements and keeping things fair and balanced, and it can help you focus your mind on what you want to say in a presentation or help you know how to stay calm in an argument. Kyanite in general is a very positive, protective stone that facilitates flow and harmony.

Try this: Carry or wear a Blue Kyanite if you need to give a presentation or speak your truth in some way.

Labradorite

Color: Blue or gray with iridescent swirls
Chakra: Throat, third eye
Zodiac: n/a

Labradorite is great for connecting you to your intuition and even psychic powers. If there's anything you're not sure of, you can use Labradorite to increase your understanding of it. It's like your own little crystal ball.

It's also really good for learning and studying, because it can sharpen your brain. Keep one near your desk while studying or doing homework.

Try this: Keep a Labradorite by your bed as you sleep, and see if you know the answer to your problem in the morning. You can also keep one near your desk where you study or do homework, or carry one in your pocket on days when you have a math test.

Lapis Lazuli
> Color: Blue with thin white or gold veins
> Chakra: Throat
> Zodiac: n/a

Lapis Lazuli is a famous stone, very popular with the ancient Egyptians. It's really good for communication and being your true self. So if you need to get in touch with who you really are, this is a great stone for you!

Try this: Carry a Lapis Lazuli in your pocket or wear it as jewelry on a day when you need to give a speech, audition for a play, or try out for a sport (if it's allowed—otherwise just keep it in your gym bag).

Lava Stone

> Color: Black, porous with holes all throughout
> Chakra: Root
> Zodiac: Taurus, Cancer

Lava Stone is a powerful grounding stone that helps you feel connected to the earth. It's literally made from lava, hence its name. The magma erupts from volcanoes, cools down into lava, and then cools down into Lava Stone. So it's literally straight from the ground. That's why it's so grounding.

Lava Stone is wonderful for soothing the nervous system and keeping you stable when you're a bit on edge. It's also great because the little holes let you use it as a diffuser if you have some essential oils to put on there!

Try this: Wear a Lava Stone bracelet and put a few drops of your favorite calming essential oils on it. The stones will smell nice all day, and you will get the benefit of the essential oils, which can be very relaxing or energizing, depending on what you need. If you need to feel calm, try lavender or patchouli. If you need to feel energized, try peppermint or lemon. Eucalyptus is good for both. Try different scents and see which helps you the most.

Lepidolite

Color: Swirls of soft purple and white

Chakra: Crown

Zodiac: Libra

Lepidolite is a wonderfully calming stone, and it's really good for sleep. If you have bad dreams or are afraid of the dark, let Lepidolite take care of that. It's a spiritually healing stone, connecting you with your angel guides (if you believe in those), or just for generally making you more awake of your connection to everyone and everything.

It's also a really calming stone. If you wake up stressed (or go to bed stressed), it can be really helpful for getting you in a Zen state of mind during one of the most important parts of your day—when you sleep.

Try this: Put a Lepidolite near your pillow at night when you sleep for gentle, peaceful dreams.

Malachite

Color: Green
Chakra: Heart
Zodiac: Capricorn

Malachite is a wonderful stone for friendship and emotional connection. It can also help you bring up deep emotions that you're holding back. In fact, it's a good stone for any relationship, so use it any time you want to balance your feelings in any way, and especially if there's someone you want to talk about your feelings with (either positive or negative).

Try this: Wear a Malachite necklace near your heart or carry one in your pocket on a day when you have a lot of feelings or if you need to share something with someone.

Mookaite

Color: Purple, red, orange, yellow, and cream swirls

Chakra: n/a

Zodiac: n/a

Mookaite comes from the Mooka River in Australia. It's a happy, positive stone that helps you feel really good in the past, present, and future. That means it's okay to be in the here and now, no need to worry or stress!

Mookaite is a great stone for confidence and positivity. Wear or carry Mookaite to help you feel uplifted and cheerful no matter what.

Try this: Wear or carry Mookaite with you to help you live life to the fullest!

Moonstone

Color: Pearly, iridescent white

Chakra: Crown, sacral

Zodiac: n/a

Moonstone is a wonderful stone for balancing emotions and feeling peaceful and calm. It's a great stone for helping you embrace change, because it's kinda like the moon itself—always changing, yet always staying the same. The flowing, wax and wane pattern of the moon is just like life, and the moonstone reflects that to a tee.

Use a Moonstone to help with meditation, reflection, and peace. It's a great stone to wear as jewelry.

Try this: Wear a Moonstone to help you find balance and peace, even when life is experiencing some ups and downs.

Obsidian

Color: Shiny black

Chakra: Root

Zodiac: Scorpio

Obsidian is a shiny black stone that comes from cooled lava. Historically it was used to make tools, such as arrowheads. Obsidian is also a powerful grounding stone, though. It's also great for protecting against negative energies.

Using Obsidian as a grounding stone is really good for a clear mind free from clutter. Carry an Obsidian with you to feel safe and strong and grounded, no matter what happens.

Try this: Carry an Obsidian with you for clear, strong mental patterns.

Opal

Color: Pearly, iridescent white
Chakra: Crown
Zodiac: n/a

Opal is a beautiful, pale stone that stands for luck, innocence, clarity, calm, and joy. It's a great stone for sleep and good dreams, and it's also great for creativity and art. You can use Opal to energize and uplift you, even while keeping you calm and at peace.

Try this: Meditate with some Opal and see what bursts of creative insight come to you.

Pearl

Color: Pearly, soft white with a gentle sheen
Chakra: Crown
Zodiac: Gemini

Pearl is a mineral, not a stone, and it's developed in the shells of oysters. You can have freshwater or saltwater pearls. Pearls represent peace and serenity and connections to the higher realms.

Try this: Wear Pearl jewelry as an elegant, tasteful way to use crystals even on the fanciest occasions. Make sure to get real Pearls and check that they are not manmade or synthetic.

Peridot

Color: Light, translucent green
Chakra: Heart
Zodiac: Leo

Peridot is a beautiful crystal of love and compassion. It's also sometimes called "the study stone" because it's great for focusing the mind! So you can use it when you want to work on homework or learning something new.

Peridot is great for balancing your emotions and your ability to give and receive. And it's a great stone for renewal, healing, and growth. It's also the birthstone for August.

Try this: Wear a Peridot when you are studying or learning a new skill or talent. You can also keep it on your desk or workspace if that's better for you.

Pyrite

Color: Gold

Chakra: Solar plexus

Zodiac: Leo

Pyrite is also known as "fool's gold" because it looks almost exactly like gold. It's not, although it's still an amazing stone with all kinds of properties. It's good for logic and confidence and making decisions. It's also good for attracting wealth, so use it if you want to focus on saving up for something big or maybe find a job opportunity. Pyrite is known as a good stone for thinking outside the box and coming up with new ideas.

Try this: Carry a Pyrite for good luck when solving problems or coming up with solutions, and keep it near you when looking for opportunities for growth.

Red Jasper

> Color: Red-orange streaked with black or brown
> Chakra: Root, sacral
> Zodiac: n/a

Red Jasper is a strong, courageous stone known for increasing bravery and determination. It's a balancing, grounding stone, as well, but not in a sleepy way—more like an "I'm unstoppable!" way. Heroes used to use swords inlaid with Red Jasper for its empowering mojo.

You can use Red Jasper to help you feel calm and settled but also courageous and strong. It can help you overcome challenges or complete difficult tasks.

Try this: Keep a Red Jasper in your pocket on the day of an important sporting event, test, or other challenge. Let it remind you that you can do whatever you set your mind to.

Rose Quartz

Color: Light, soft pink with white veins

Chakra: Heart

Zodiac: Libra, Taurus

Rose quartz is the stone of unconditional love. It helps you feel connected, supported, and loved no matter what you or anyone else does or says. You can love yourself and love other people better when there's a Rose Quartz around.

You can carry it in your pocket or wear it as jewelry, especially on days when you might need a little extra courage to love yourself more.

Try this: Keep a Rose Quartz near your heart during the day for optimum unconditional love. Especially useful on a date, at a funeral, or during difficult times.

Ruby (raw and gemstone)
>Color: Red
>Chakra: Root, heart
>Zodiac: n/a

Ruby is the stone of power and passion. It's great for helping you get excited about life! It's also really good if you're feeling sensitive or emotional. It can help you understand and appreciate your emotions and sensitivities, while balancing anything that might be a lot for you to handle at the moment.

Use Ruby to help with motivation and excitement whenever you are feeling bored, unmotivated, or just not really caring about anything right now. It's a great stone to help you get a "spark" for the things you love!

Try this: Hold a Ruby while you lie down quietly for a few minutes. Let yourself feel soothed and balanced, and then go back to your day with increased confidence and energy.

Sapphire

Color: Blue

Chakra: Throat, third eye

Zodiac: Virgo

Sapphires are stones of wisdom. They can help you with mental clarity, understanding others and yourself, and knowing your own mind—even if other people disagree with you. It's a very calming, healing stone that helps you communicate and think clearly, so it's great to have around at any time.

Sapphire can bring peace, tranquility, and balance. It's also really gorgeous to look at, so wearing it as jewelry is always fun and exciting! It's a good stone for growing up, so a day when you are transitioning to the next phase of your life (such as graduation or driver's ed) is a good day for Sapphire, too.

Try this: Wear a Sapphire on a day when you need to make lots of decisions (or one important one) or when you have lots you need to learn or memorize, or whenever you need a little more wisdom in your life.

Selenite

Color: Translucent white

Chakra: Crown

Zodiac: Taurus, Gemini

Selenite is possibly the most cleansing stone. It's best for cleansing other stones and can ward off negativity—mental, emotional, physical, and spiritual. Keeping selenite by your bed is a great option for peaceful dreams, clear thinking, and just all-around good vibes.

It's a stone of purity, clarity, and peace. It's also a great stone for forgiveness and healing. Keep a Selenite in your pocket, backpack, or bag to have these properties with you all day.

Try this: Use a Selenite "wand" (or just any piece of Selenite) as a cleanser for your room or your aura. If your room or you feel a little unsettled or off-kilter, wave the Selenite over the space or over your body to cleanse out any bad vibes clinging to you or that spot. Then pay attention to how you feel—I always feel instantly lighter!

Shungite
Color: Shiny grayish-black
Chakra: Root
Zodiac: n/a

Shungite is named after the one place in the world you can find it: a village called Shunga in Russia. No one is quite sure how it came to be there, either— some say it might have been from a meteorite a long, long time ago. Some people use Shungite to purify water and protect against EMF radiations, which are the electronic waves sent out by Wi-Fi routers. If you want to try using them this way, be sure and ask an adult to help you research first!

Otherwise, Shungite is an amazing root chakra stone that helps you feel grounded and calm. It's an amazing stone for protection from negativity, so holding or wearing Shungite can be a great way to soothe any frazzled nerves.

Try this: Wear or carry Shungite with you throughout your day to help keep you grounded and calm.

Smoky Quartz

Color: Translucent gray, brown, and white swirls

Chakra: Root

Zodiac: n/a

Smoky Quartz is a great detoxer for negativity. In fact, it can turn negativity into positivity! Putting some smoky quartz around your room is a great way to keep it feeling light and positive. It's also a really grounding stone, so it can help keep you feeling supported and relaxed. If you feel stuck or over-whelmed by a situation, Smoky Quartz can be a great stone to help you get "un-stuck" and moving in a positive direction.

Try this: Keep a Smoky Quartz in your favorite relaxing spot to keep it clear of negativity and help you recharge from a stressful day.

Sodalite
Color: Deep blue with white marbling
Chakra: Throat, third eye
Zodiac: Sagittarius

Sodalite is a powerful stone of truth, especially knowing and understanding your true self. And then, of course, living as your true self! It's also good for balancing emotions and articulating them clearly. Sodalite is a highly logical stone that's great for creativity and understanding, so it's a big helper when you've got difficult homework or want to try out a new self-identity for a while.

Try this: Wear or carry Sodalite to help you focus on being relaxed, calm, confident, and self-assured, especially when it comes to knowing and understanding yourself.

Tiger's Eye

Color: Yellow, brown, and black stripes

Chakra: Solar plexus

Zodiac: Leo

Tiger's Eye represents courage and making good decisions. Wear a Tiger's Eye close to your solar plexus when you need to give a presentation or make a big decision, especially if it's one you need to find the answer to by looking within (instead of going with what everyone else thinks). As a power stone, Tiger's Eye is an all-around great stone for whenever you need to feel courageous.

Try this: Carry a Tiger's Eye in your pocket or wear it as a necklace when you need extra courage in your life.

Topaz
Color: Light translucent blue
Chakra: Throat
Zodiac: n/a

Topaz is a great stone for clear communication and relieving any emotional tension. In fact, if you have a headache due to stress, lying down and meditating with some Topaz might help you relax. It can also help you understand your feelings better, so having some nearby while journaling about your feelings is a good idea.

It's also good for honesty, understanding, and insight (those little "ah ha!" moments where you learn something about life or something in it).

Try this: Journal with some Topaz nearby to help you focus on your feelings and what they really mean in the grand scheme of things.

Turquoise
>Color: Light blue-green with black veins
>Chakra: Throat
>Zodiac: n/a

Turquoise is a highly popular stone for jewelry, so it's an excellent stone for all kinds of uses. It's a great stone for calming, balancing, and brightening the emotions.

It's a bright, cheerful stone that also helps you feel poised and at peace, even while it promotes luck and positive feelings. Wear some Turquoise jewelry on a regular basis to increase your overall mood and bring yourself into alignment with yourself and anyone else you might want to connect with.

Try this: Wear Turquoise to help you feel positive and upbeat without being too spastic.

Violet Fluorite

Color: Violet

Chakra: Third eye, crown

Zodiac: n/a

Also sometimes called Purple Fluorite, Violet Fuorite is known as "the genius stone" because it helps your mental powers so much. It can help with mental confusion, like when you feel "foggy" and tired, and it's great for helping you focus.

It's also a great stone for peace and calm and can be helpful for sleep. Violet Fluorite aligns the body, mind, and spirit so they are in harmony with one another.

Try this: Use Violet Fluorite in a grid with some other good mental clarity and sleep crystals. Keep it near your bed so your sleeping area can be a great place to chill out, meditate, and have really calming dreams.

CHAPTER 9

CRYSTAL MEDITATIONS THAT CAN CHANGE YOUR LIFE

By now you're no longer a beginner! So it's time to go a little deeper.

I mentioned in an earlier chapter that meditations with crystals are the simplest and quickest way to access the magic stored up in your crystals. Simply holding a crystal in your hand and taking a deep breath counts as a meditation. That's a great place to start, but let's take it to the next level.

In this chapter I have "scripts" for three crystal meditations. There are millions of ways to do these meditations, and I hope you start to create them for yourself! But for now, I'm going to walk you through three of my favorites. (I use these all the time; they really make me feel great.)

· · ·

So how do these scripts work? Well, there are lots of options.

You can do these by yourself. Just follow the directions and read the statements out loud. Don't be shy! But maybe lock your door so no one walks in on you during your practice.

Another option is with friends! If you have a crystal friend, have her/him/them read the script to you. This can be an intense way to bond. And what a gift to give your friends!

And finally, if you get the audiobook version of this book, the narrator will read these to you! With soothing music to fit the mood. All you have to do is sit back and listen!

MEDITATION #1

Choose a stone that represents the third eye (Amethyst or Howlite, for instance) or crown chakras (how about Clear Quartz or Opal?) and get ready to meditate. We will work on feeling mentally calm, clear, and safe by letting the crystal soothe your mental health. Don't forget to cleanse the crystal when you are done!

Start to relax, lying down on your back if that's best for you today, or perhaps on your side or sitting up if that's better. Notice how your body is feeling and adjust it as needed. As you start to relax just a little bit more, I invite you to take your chosen stone and place it on your fore-head, if that feels comfortable to you. You can also place it near your head, on your lap, or anywhere else you choose.

Take a deep, calming breath, counting to four as you do so. Hold that breath while you count to four. Now, exhale slowly, also counting to four. Hold your breath at the bottom of the exhale, once again counting to four. Keep this steady, even rhythm as you continue to breathe: four in, hold for four, four out, hold for four. Again, four in, hold for four, four out, hold for four. Good.

. . .

Keep breathing to the count of four, and start to notice how your mind feels. Notice any thoughts that come to your mind—just notice them. There's no need to pay them any attention. Acknowledge them, and keep focusing on your breath.

Keep breathing in this gentle pattern as you begin to focus on the crystal, resting on or near your forehead. Notice how it feels. Is it cool or warm? Heavy or light? What else can you sense about the crystal? Focus on the crystal, and don't forget to breathe.

Now, imagine that the crystal is absorbing any negative thought patterns or beliefs in your mind. Allow the crystal to act like a nice big "eraser" for all the stuff that happened today, perhaps at school or at home or with your friends or wherever else you went today. Let the crystal erase all the negative thoughts, the fears, the worry, the judgment of yourself or others. Release it all, and just focus on your breath.

Check in with your mind again. Notice your thoughts, just see how they are doing. No need to pay them any attention, just acknowledge them and go back to your breath.

. . .

You can stay here as long as you wish, allowing your breath and the crystal to work together to help you feel calm and relaxed. You can do this meditation any time of the day or night, whenever you need a mental health boost. Take as long as you need, and then allow your breath to return to normal, open your eyes, and go back to the rest of your day.

MEDITATION #2

Choose your favorite heart chakra stone (perhaps an Emerald, Malachite, Bloodstone, Ruby, Rose Quartz, or similar) for this meditation and get ready to focus! You will want to be sure to cleanse your crystal after this meditation is over.

Whenever you are ready, I invite you to find yourself in a comfortable position, perhaps lying on your back or reclining in a chair. If it's available to you, I invite you to place the stone on your chest, near your heart chakra.

Today we are going to allow three emotions to come up for healing. Sometimes we store emotions in our body instead of fully feeling them. It's okay if you do this for the short term, but over a long time, this can result in extra stress or even health issues. So taking the time to process our old emotions can be really comforting.

First, let's focus on our breath. Since we will be processing emotions today, it's very important that we stay calm and connected to our breath. Take a deep breath in and hold it for a moment. Good. Now, slowly release your breath in one long, easy woosh. Well done.

• • •

Take another deep, cleansing breath. Hold it in, just for a moment, then release all your breath in one big breath. Good job.

Just one more time: deep, slow breath, hold it, and... release. Excellent work.

Now, allow your breath to come back to a steady, even rhythm. Notice how it feels to breathe in through your nose, out through your nose. Notice how the air feels cool and light on its way in. Notice how warm it feels on its way out. You might also notice that you're already feeling a bit lighter, a bit more calm and still.

If your mind starts to wander during this meditation, that is okay. Just gently guide it back to the rhythm of your breath. Breath in, breath out. Breath in, breath out.

Start to notice how your feet feel. Wiggle them a little if you need to, get a little more comfortable. Just notice if your feet are hot or cold, tense or relaxed. And keep focusing on your breath. Breath in, breath out. Breath in, breath out.

. . .

Now notice your hands. Adjust them if they want to move, notice if they're hot or cold or calm or tense. Just keep focusing on each and every breath. Breath in, breath out. Breath in, breath out.

Now notice if you hear anything around you. Are there any sounds nearby? Just notice them. Notice how they reach your eardrums. Notice anything else you can hear; perhaps you can hear your heartbeat. Or the sound of your breath. Keep noticing your breathing. Breath in, breath out. Breath in, breath out.

Your breath is your anchor. Whenever you get a little tossed around on the storms of life, your breath can bring you right back to feeling calm, centered, and supported. Breath in, breath out. Breath in, breath out.

And now, continuing to notice your breath, we can start by bringing our awareness to that stone you placed on your chest. We're going to allow one emotion at a time to come up and focus on each one at a time. If another emotion tries to intrude, remind it that its turn will come shortly. With just your thoughts, you can decide what to pay attention to.

. . .

So, let's try Emotion Number 1. What are you feeling right now? Let's not try to name the emotion just yet. For now, just notice that you are feeling something. There is no need to decide if this is a "good" emotion or a "bad" emotion. For now, it's just an emotion. And it is safe to feel it. Keep noticing your breath. Breath in, breath out. Breath in, breath out.

Let's try to understand this emotion a little more. Even if you aren't sure what the emotion is, ask yourself if it has a color. What color is this emotion?

Now, ask if it has a shape. What shape is this emotion? Does it have hard edges? Or soft? Fuzzy? Or sharp? Smooth? Or rough? Notice anything else about the shape of this emotion.

And lastly, ask if the emotion has a weight. Is it heavy? Or light? Strong? Or thin? Just notice how this emotion feels.

Okay, let's see if we can name this emotion now. Are you feeling a little sad? Or scared? Or angry? Just notice the emotion, and try to give it a name. If it's two emotions combined, that's okay too. And if you still can't name it, that's all right. You've already done some very important work here.

Next, let's focus on Emotion Number 2. What are you feeling right now? Don't try to name the emotion just yet, don't decide if it's good or bad. Just keep noticing your breath. Breath in, breath out. Breath in, breath out.

Let's try to understand this second emotion a little more. What color is this emotion?

Now what shape is this emotion? Does it have hard edges? Or soft? Fuzzy? Or sharp? Smooth? Or rough? Notice the shape of this emotion.

And lastly, ask if the emotion has a weight. Is it heavy? Or light? Strong? Or thin? Notice how this emotion feels.

Okay, try to name this emotion now. Just notice the emotion, and try to give it a name. If it's two emotions combined, that's okay too. And if you still can't name it, that's all right. The crystal on your chest is helping you understand and process it, no matter its name.

. . .

Let's do one more. Allow yourself to feel Emotion Number 3. Don't try to name it yet. Just keep noticing your breath. Breath in, breath out. Breath in, breath out.

Let's try to understand this emotion a little more. What color is this emotion?

Now, what shape is this emotion? Does it have hard edges? Or soft? Fuzzy? Or sharp? Smooth? Or rough? Notice the shape of this emotion.

And lastly, ask if the emotion has a weight. Is it heavy? Or light? Strong? Or thin? Notice how this emotion feels.

Okay, try to name this emotion now. Just notice, and breathe.

These three emotions are no longer weighing you down. You have taken the time to honor and acknowledge them, so you can let them go, if you choose. If you need to hang on to some of them for a bit longer, that is okay.

Just like your breath, emotions come and go. Breath in, breath out. Emotions in, emotions out.

Now I invite you to imagine a glowing, green light, radiating out from that crystal lying on your chest. See that growing, green light get bigger and bigger, expanding with every breath in and every breath out.

The glowing, green light is so big that it covers your entire chest and stomach. As the light gets bigger and bigger, you start to notice how light and happy you feel. You are feeling very calm, very peaceful, and very light.

The light is so big that it covers your shoulders and arms, as well as your legs. You start to feel calmer and happier with each breath.

The green circle of light is so big now that it covers your entire body, from the top of your head to the tips of your toes. Rest here, and breathe, noticing how light and calm and happy you feel. That glowing, green light feels safe and supportive and very, very calm.

. . .

Spend a little time now, as long as you want, allowing your heart chakra crystal to help you process any more emotions that are ready to heal today. If you feel like crying or laughing or shouting, that's all right. Just let the process happen, and allow the crystal to support you in feeling better. When you're ready to go back to the rest of your day, you will know.

And remember, you can always return to your breath, any time of the day or night.

MEDITATION #3

For this meditation, choose a root chakra stone (perhaps a Shungite, Lava Stone, Hematite, Smoky Quartz, or similar). You can choose more than one stone if you wish. We will focus on grounding so you can be as calm and centered as possible while still feeling powerful and strong. Don't forget to cleanse your crystal when you are done!

As you begin to settle in to a comfortable seated or lying down position, I invite you to place your stone (or stones) on your lap, near your hips, or near your waist, wherever feels good to you today.

Notice your breath, how it feels on its way in through your nose, out through your nose. Notice its temperature, cool air moving in, warm air moving out.

Now notice your breath in your chest, how your chest rises and falls with each breath in and each breath out. Your shoulders might move with each inhale and exhale. Adjust them if needed and keep noticing the rise and fall of your chest. Notice how your ribcage expands with each breath in and each breath out.

• • •

Notice your breath in your lower belly. All the way down in your lower belly, notice how your belly expands with each breath in and contracts with each breath out. Like a bright red balloon, your belly expands and contracts, expands and contracts. Even your lower back expands as you breathe deeply, right into the very lowest point of your belly.

Notice where you have placed the crystal (or crystals). Notice how you might already be feeling just a little calmer.

Now I invite you to imagine that powerful roots, like the roots of a tall oak tree, are growing out of the bottom of your left foot and your right foot. Imagine these roots growing through the ground beneath you, down, down, down until they reach the center of the Earth. The roots grow all the way down until they reach the center of the Earth, and you are feeling safe, calm, and secure. If you need to move for any reason, the roots will move with you. You are feeling safe, calm, and secure.

Now imagine these powerful roots expanding until they are growing out of the backs of your legs, too. Out of the backs of both legs, you've got strong, powerful oak roots grounding you into the Earth below. The roots stretch all the way to the center of the Earth. You are breathing into your lower belly, your crystal is here with you, and you are feeling powerful and strong.

Now the roots continue to grow, until they are connected to your knees, thighs, and hips.

The roots keep growing, until they connect with your lower back, your middle back, your upper back. The roots stretch downward from your left arm and your right, your elbows, wrists, and hands. You can move them at any time, and you are feeling strong, powerful, and safe.

The roots now grow from your shoulders, neck, and head. Your entire body is one big mass of roots, which stretch all the way to the center of the Earth. You are totally safe, totally secure, totally connected. Breathe all the way down into your lower belly, and notice your crystal.

Take a few more breaths here.

And whenever you are ready, start to see the roots loosen their hold on the Earth beneath you. Let the roots loosen their hold on your head and neck, your shoulders, arms, and hands. Breathe into your lower belly, feel free to wiggle your hands if that feels good, shake off any extra roots.

Now see the roots loosening their hold on your upper back, middle back, and lower back. Move or stretch anything that wants to move or stretch, and keep breathing into your lower belly.

Now see the roots loosening their hold on your hips, thighs, knees, and feet. Shake your legs and feet as needed, and see the last little bits of the roots let go.

Turn onto one side or the other if you feel like it, holding on to your crystal for a few more minutes if you want to, just noticing how you feel. You can stay here as long as you wish, just breathing. And if you ever want to call upon those roots again, they will always be there whenever you need them.

CONCLUSION

At the very beginning of this book, I shared that one of my favorite parts about being a crystal girl is how aware it's made me about the world around me. Before, I thought crystals were just rocks. And they are. But they are so much *more* than rocks.

After learning about the scientific side of crystals, I started to notice how everything in the world has its own frequency, and that started to make me think. I started to think about the positivity in the world, as well as the negative. Instead of seeing everything as just, well, things...I started to see them come alive. You don't have to believe in magic or unicorns to believe in crystals. You can just believe in the energy found in everything in the universe. Or you can believe in unicorns, too. It doesn't matter.

The point is that crystals teach us to look beyond what we can see or touch. We can feel things that we can't explain, and that's okay. We can spend time out in nature and feel connected, comforted, supported. And we can take a little piece of nature with us wherever we go.

Crystals also teach us that we are each powerful. Since everything in the world has its own vibration, so do we. And we can use that powerful vibration to make a real impact. To make a difference with the life we've been given.

Haley is so good at this. This is just *one* of the reasons I admire her so much (on top of her being so cool, of course). Haley sees everything as filled with love and light and potential. And she shares that love and light wherever she goes. She has good days and bad days, of course. So do I. We all do. But when we see ourselves as connected to everything, it's really powerful. And it makes a difference.

I hope, now that you've learned a little bit about crystals, that you can do the same. Now that you've read one crystal book, you can start to read a lot more! And you can learn about other ways of making this planet a happier, safer place to live. This planet is in our hands. You are one of the smart, talented, exciting people who get to make it an amazing place to be!

Thanks for coming along with me and Haley in this book. We've loved having you here. Now, go out and use your new crystal knowledge. You know what to do.

REVIEW THE BOOK

Hi friends,

I hope you enjoyed CRYSTALS AND GEMSTONE FOR KIDS AND TEENS! I would be incredibly grateful if you would take 60 seconds to leave a review for this book. Even if it's just a few sentences.... It really helps people find it.

Leave a review at : https://www.amazon.com/review/create-review/?ie=UTF8&channel=glance-detail&asin=B0B1M1BN2Z

Or scan this QR code:

Thank you so much!!

RESOURCES

https://www.gia.edu/rose-quartz-history-lore

https://www.elledecor.com/life-culture/fun-at-home/g9606722/healing-crystals/

https://astrostyle.com/crystal-horoscope/

Made in United States
North Haven, CT
25 October 2022

25893408R00085